"If you truly love nature, you will find beauty everywhere."

Vincent van Gogh

Ant

arduous worker
able-bodied soldier
authentic insect with head
abdomen, head and thorax
abide in social colonies

carpenter ant…*camponotus pennsylvanicus,* ¼ - ½"

Bumble Bee

buzzing flower to flower
busy pollinator
bright yellow and black
bows to Queen mother of all

bumble bee...*bombus fervidus, ½ - ¾"*

Cicada

clicks for a mate
cacophony of chirping
cyclical, every 7, 13 or 17 years
calls like a circular saw cutting wood

cicada, dog-day harvestfly…*tibicen canicularis, 1 – 1 1/4"*

Dragonfly

darting
dancing
dazzling
damselflies
"devil's darning needle"
downs mosquitoes

black saddlebag dragonfly…*tramea lacerata, 1 ¾ - 2 1/8"*

Earwig

eerie pincers
egg-layer
evening dweller in dusty corners
enchanting

European earwig...*forficula auricularia, 3/8 – 5/8"*

Firefly

flasher of bioluminescence
flitters on warm humid nights
festive light show of communication
flickers to lure a mate

firefly...*photuris pensylvanica, ¼ - 3/8"*

Grasshopper

grazes voraciously
great jumper
giant hind legs
grassy-colored of green and straw

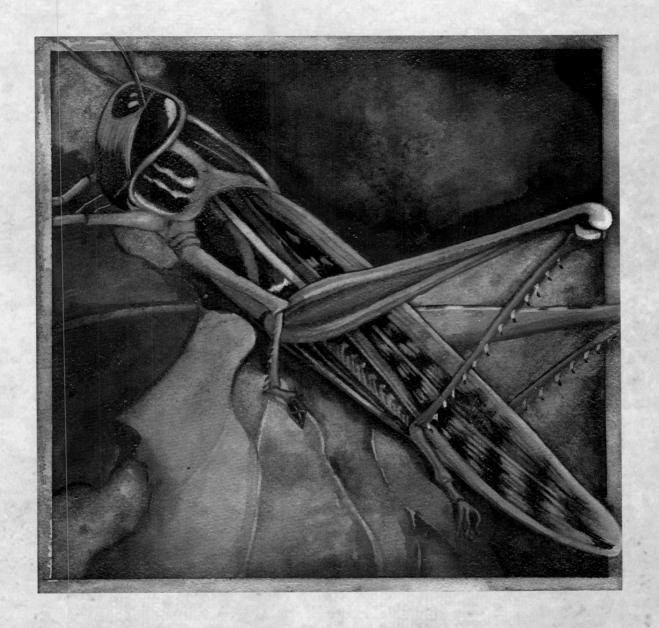

American grasshopper...*schistocerca Americana, 1 ½ - 2 5/8"*

Housefly

hungry
host to disease
"halteres" are second set of wings
helpful pollinators

housefly… *musca domestica, 1/8 – ¼"*

Isia Isabella

inches as "woolly bear caterpillar"
identified by its black and bands
inky black bands tell age not severity of winter
isia will become a black spotted orange moth

isia isabella, woolly caterpillar...*ixodes pacificus, 1 – 2 1/8"*

June Beetle

just eats pine needles
jeweled elytra, wing covers
jade-colored stripes
just emerges in late June and July

ten-lined June beetle...*polyphylla decemlimeata*, ¼ - 1 ¼"

Katydid

kin to grasshopper
kooky long antennae
kress-green color
"kaydid" she chirps

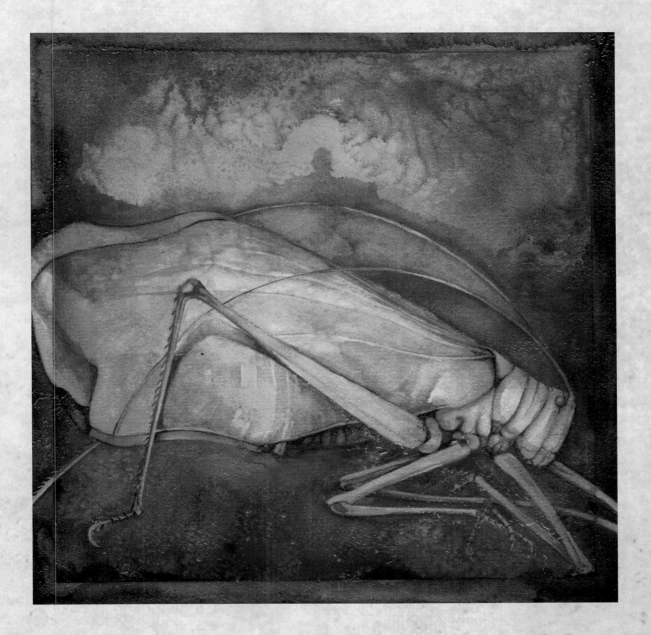

true kaydid…*pterophylla camellifolia, 1 3/8 – 2 1/8”*

Ladybug

loves eating lime-green aphids
lolly-pop red elytron wing covers
lamp black spots
larvae are black or gray
lots or just 2 spots

convergent lady beetle…*hippodamia convergens, 1/8 – ¼"*

Mosquito

males suck plant juice
malaria is transmitted by mosquito
merry females suck blood from mammals
magnificent proboscis, nose, is very long

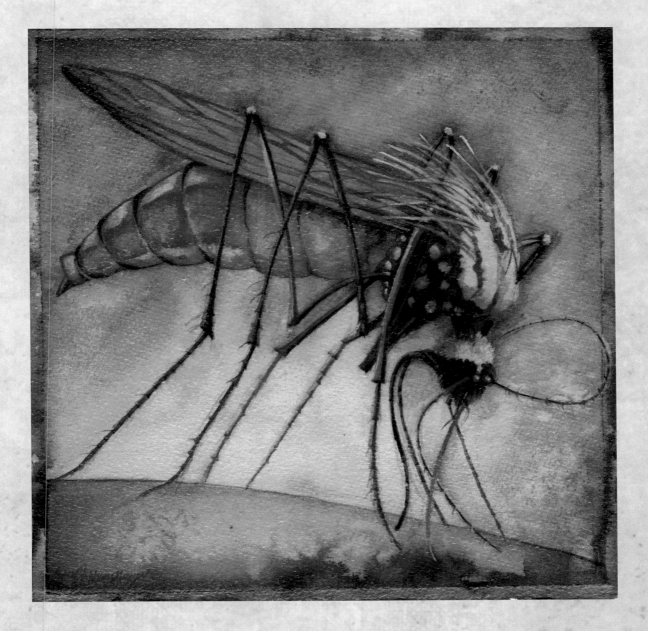

winter mosquito…*culiseta inornata*, ¼ - ½"

No-see-um

nest in salt ponds and coastal marshes
naturally, females feed on blood
note feeding at dawn and dusk
nasty, pesky "punkies"

no-see-um…*culicoides, 1/18"*

Orbweaver Spider

orchestrates beautiful webs
orangish-white silk egg sacs
owns eight eyes
oval-shaped body
only an arachnid spider, not an insect

orchard orbweaver spider…*leucauge venusta, 1/8 – ¼"*

Praying Mantis

prominent forelegs
prayer-like position
prey on anything they catch
particular females even eat their mate
pivots head 360 degrees
"papier-mache" quality is their nest
protected by a hard coating, the nest repels birds

praying mantis…*mantis religiosa, 2 – 2 ½"*

Question Mark Caterpillar

quirky creature
quick to feed on the elm
question mark on moth wing

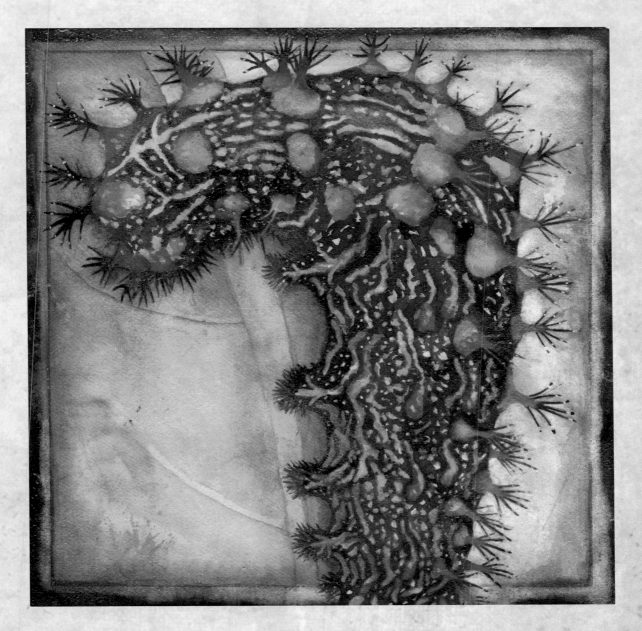

question mark caterpillar…*polygonia interrogationis, 2"*

Roly Poly

rolls in ball for protection
really harmless bug
re-named "stink bug" by some
resembles an armadillo's armor

roly poly…*armadillidium vulgare, to ¾"*

Silverfish

sneaks in warm, humid spaces
scurrying silverfish do not swim
silently searches for crumbs and microbes
slithers at night in corners and crevices
shell-like body

silverfish…*lepisma saccharina, 3/8 – ½"*

Tick

tenacious biters
taste for blood-filled mammals
transmit diseases like Lyme
tiny nymphs feed on white-footed mice
ticks are not insects
therefore ticks are an arachnid, spider family with 8 legs

black-legged tick…*ixodes scapularis, up to 1/8"*

Underwing Moth

under the wings it's red, pink, and black
utter nothing but attracted to light
unusual feathered antennae
under dark of night they fly, nocturnal
underwings called "amatrix"

sweetheart underwing …*catocala amatrix, 3 –3 3/8"*

Viceroy Butterfly

very similar to the monarch
variant is black band on hindwing
victorious by its distaste to predators
vibrant orange color

viceroy butterfly…*limenitis archippus, 2 5/8 – 3"*

Walkingstick

worldwide 3000 species of sticks
wingless sticks, herbivores, feed on plants
"woody" adults live weeks to a few months
would be mistaken for a branch
wonder in its motionless pause

walkingstick…*diapheromera femorata, 2 1/8 – 2 5/8"*

Xystodesmid Millipede

xenophobic, they hide during the day
xystodesmids produce benzaldehyde and hydrogen cyanide
x-tremely distasteful secretions emit odor of almond or cherry

xystodesmid millipede…*apheloria tigana, to 2 ¼"*

Yellow Jacket

yellow stripes on abdomen
yellow jackets are very social
yield to a division of labor
yikes, can sting more than once

yellow jacket...*vespula,* ½ - 5/8"

Zebra Swallowtail

zips through woodlands, in search of paw paws
zealously sucks nectar from flowers
zebras have a long proboscis, tongue
zigs and zags with great beauty

zebra swallowtail...*eurytides Marcellus, 2 3/8 – 3 ½"*

"The most beautiful thing we can experience is the mysterious. It is the source of all true art and science."

Albert Einstein

It started with the yellow jacket wasp I found in the street. Even though it was dead, the wasp had an animated, cartoon-like quality. I carefully cradled it in my hand and was immediately inspired to paint it.

Soon I noticed other insects: Cicada were emerging, leaving their scarab-like shells behind. Dragonflies were hovering about my head. I collected what I found and my insect treasures mounted – firefly, butterfly, beetle, ladybug and more, arousing my inner scientist. The local library and bookstore provided me with a trove of compelling facts and educational information. My paintings and learning formed a journal of bugs and insects and I organized them from a to z. I wanted to hold a special book in my hand recognizing the beauty of nature I had discovered. So I created this volume, "Abecedarian Insectarium, Bugs and Insects A to Z".

Lynn Stephens Massey grew up throughout the country— in Louisville and Shelbyville Kentucky; Dallas, San Diego and Portland, Oregon.
Childhood gave her a range of arts as well: Her mother was a visual artist and her father a musician, a tenor.
Stephens chose the visual arts as her career, pursuing a degree in graphic design at PNCA in Portland, Oregon; illustration at Art Center in Pasadena, California; and painting at Ecole des Beaux-Arts in Paris, France. Stephens combines her life experience and art and lives richly, drawing, painting and playing the piano in her home in Connecticut.

Printed in the United States
By Bookmasters